Bibliographic information published by the German National Library:

The German National Library lists this publication in the National Bibliography; detailed bibliographic data are available on the Internet at http://dnb.dnb.de .

Imprint:

Copyright © 2019 GRIN Verlag
Print and binding: Books on Demand GmbH, Norderstedt Germany
ISBN: 9783668981317

This book at GRIN:

https://www.grin.com/document/491172

Michelle Bettendorf

Aus der Reihe: e-fellows.net stipendiaten-wissen

e-fellows.net (Hrsg.)

Band 3121

Keyboard Alarm System

The Creation of a Microprocessor System Using Arduino

GRIN Verlag

GRIN - Your knowledge has value

Since its foundation in 1998, GRIN has specialized in publishing academic texts by students, college teachers and other academics as e-book and printed book. The website www.grin.com is an ideal platform for presenting term papers, final papers, scientific essays, dissertations and specialist books.

Visit us on the internet:

http://www.grin.com/

http://www.facebook.com/grincom

http://www.twitter.com/grin_com

Keyboard alarm system

Michelle Tina Bettendorf

This project is made under the course
Embedded Systems

Automation and Calculations
Politehnica University Timisoara
Romania
June 2019

Contents

1 Abstract

A microprocessor system project using Arduino was created in order to build an alarm system for the keyboard of a computer.

The alarm system consists of blinking LEDs, sound, taking a picture of the unauthorized person, sending that image per email, login when and what that person is doing, a distraction system and also the opportunity to stop the alarm through a password.

Keywords: Arduino, Embedded system, microcontroller, alarm system, security

2 Introduction

Almost every student knows the following situation. They study in the library or in the study room and then they have to leave the study room for a few minutes to go to get a fresh coffee, refill their water bottle or to go to the bathroom. But what to do with the laptop? Leaving it unsupervised for a few minutes? What happens if someone comes and tries to use it? Also at work what happens with the computer while leaving the working place for a few minutes? Can it be that someone tries to get some information from it by trying to hack the password? Also at work sometimes you can't even lock the computer, what to do when you have to leave the office for a short time?

For these scenarios I'll present in the following pages a solution. How about a little system next to the computer checking if someone puts their fingers on the keyboard. These little systems looks like a little work project, so it wouldn't be too obvious. It does not only make an alarm, which consists of noise and blinking, it also takes a picture of the thief with the integrated camera of the computer and sends it immediately to your mail-address, so that you can react fast. Furthermore a protocol is saved with the date and time, when it happened and which processes were open at that time, so what the person could see. On top of that a distraction system is starting as soon as the unauthorized person tries to do something on the computer. This distraction system consists of opening multiple programs and pictures. Of course it is possible to stop the alarm by typing on the console the right password.

3 Hardware

This project is designed out of the Arduino UNO R3 Starter Kit. The components used from this kit are: one Arduino UNO R3, one Ultrasonic sensor, one red LED, one yellow LED, one pipo sensor, 2 330R Resistors and 9 wires
The build circuit looks like this:

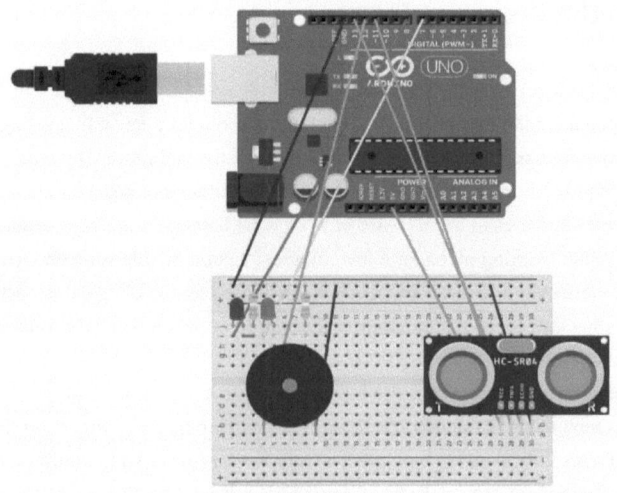

Figure 1   author's own work

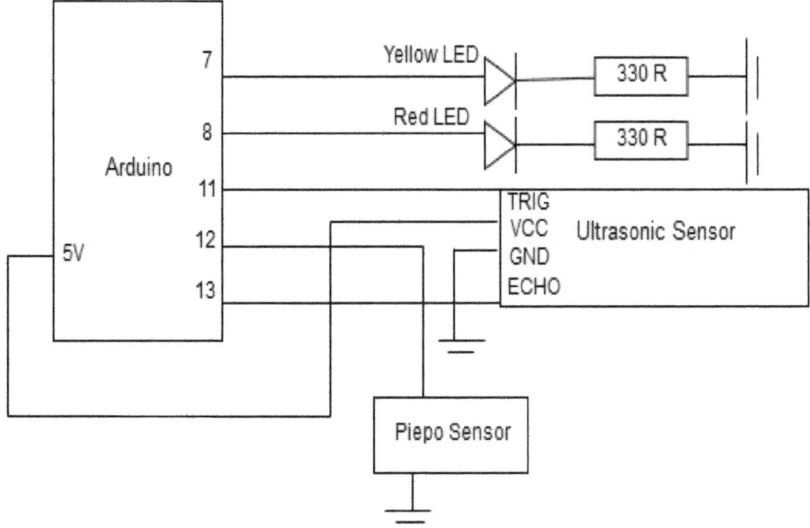

Figure 2   author's own work

4   Software

The Software consists of an Arduino and a C# part. The Arduino part was made
with the Arduino IDE. The C# part was made with Visual Studio.

4.1   Arduino

The Arduino part consists of the detection of the distance and reacting towards
it. By using serial communication on the 9600 Baud rate, it gives a signal to the
C# part to take action. Furthermore it listens if a stop signal from the C# part is
coming and exits the program, if this is the case. Also in the Arduino part is the
alarm consisting of LEDs and sound programmed.

4.2   C#

The C# part consists of a bit more than the Arduino part. In this part more things are happening. The picture is taken, the mail is sent, the distraction system goes on and the protocol is written.

The first thing to do in this part is the serial communication. For this are Threads used. The Threads are necessary for the part of stopping the alarm. Without them the program would wait for a user input and not doing the alarm program. The picture is taken through the webcam from the computer and saved in a specific folder on the PC. Also another class is just for the webcam. In this class the AForge library is included. This class is not only made for taking a picture, it already has some methods for doing an extension for using not only the camera of the computer. As a summary it is a class for using cameras connected to the computer.

For the sending the mail, the mail-address of the user is needed and also the account log in data. Furthermore is the Port and the SMTP-Server-address from the used mail portal needed. In this case is Yahoo used. Furthermore I used in this program my own mail-address, which the account log in data and mail-address will not be in the code below. So there will be a blank space, where originally this data was filled in.

For the distraction system are some processes, which were already on my computer, used. This can be changed individually. Also which pictures are opened, can be changed. I used some non-important landscapes pictures. As programs I opened in this case notepad++, Microsoft Word, Microsoft Excel and Microsoft Powerpoint. These programs have all different sizes as a preset, when they are opened, that's why I chose them. For the protocol is another class and one method in the main class used. The class is for writing in a text file. The method is used to detect all the processes and to remove all the common background processes. Furthermore is the date and time detected and written with the used processes in the protocol text file.

4.3 Used APIs

Arduino:
· Servo.h
C#:
· System
· System.IO
· System.IO.Ports
· System.Diagnostics
· System.Net.Mail
· System.Windows.Media.Imaging
· ImageCapture
· System.Drawing
· System.Security
· System.Threading
· System.Drawing.Imaging
· System.Drawing.Image
· System.Drawing
· AForge.Video
· AForge.Video.DirectShow
· System.Collections.Generic
· System.Linq
· System.Text
· System.Threading.Tasks

5 Results and further work

Results:
· Detection of usage of the keyboard through the ultrasonic sensor
· Alarm consisting of blinking LEDs and sound made of the Piepo-Sensor
· Distraction and not ability of using the PC for one minute by opening programs
and pictures

· Taking a snapshot of the person trying to use the computer

· Sending an alarm mail to an preset mail-adress with an attachment of the token snapshot

· Stopping the alarm with a password

· Protocol with date, time and used processes stored on the desktop

Further work:

· Using face recognition for not triggering the alarm if it's the user · Showing a live stream from the camera with a text underneath, that this incident is reported

6   Code

6.1   Arduino

```
#include <Servo.h>
#define ECHO_PIN 11
double distance = 100;
double time;
int rled = 8; //Pin Red LED
int yled = 7; //Pin Yellow LED
int buzz = 12; //PIN Passive Buzzer
int trigger = 13; //Pin Ultrasonic Sensor
int echo = 11;
int frequency = 600; //Frequency
int lesen = 0;
String password = "1";

void setup() {
  pinMode(rled, OUTPUT);
  pinMode(yled, OUTPUT);
  Serial.begin(9600);
  pinMode(trigger, OUTPUT);
  pinMode(echo, INPUT);
```

```
}

void loop() {

  // measuring the distance
  delay(1000);

  /* shortly no voltage, so that later with sending the trigger
   * signal is clear
   */
  digitalWrite(trigger, LOW);
  delay(5);
  digitalWrite(trigger, HIGH); //sending the ultrasonic wave
  delay(10);
  digitalWrite(trigger, LOW); //stopping sending the signal

  /* with the command pulse-in is the time counted till the
     ultrasonic wave
   * returns
   */
  time = pulseIn(echo, HIGH);
  distance = (time/2) * 0.03432;
  delay(1000);

  //starting the alarm, if the distance is smaller than 30
  if (distance < 30)
  {
    while(true)
    {
      //writing that the alarm begins
      for(int i = 0; i < 10; i++)
      {
      Serial.write("ALARM");
      Serial.println();
```

```
//starting the sound and LEDs
tone(12,frequency);

for(int i = 0; i < 10; i++)
{
  frequency = 1500;
  digitalWrite(rled,LOW);
  digitalWrite(yled, HIGH);
  delay(100);
  frequency = 600;
  digitalWrite(rled,HIGH);
  digitalWrite(yled,LOW);
  delay(100);
}

//turning of the alarm
lesen = Serial.read();
Serial.print(lesen);
delay(1000);
if(lesen != -1)
{
  digitalWrite(rled,LOW);
  digitalWrite(yled,LOW);
  frequency = 0;
  exit(0);
}
}
}
}
}
```

6.2   C#

```csharp
using ImageCapture;
using System;
using System.Collections;
using System.Diagnostics;
using System.Drawing;
using System.Drawing.Imaging;
using System.IO;
using System.IO.Ports;
using System.Net.Mail;
using System.Security;
using System.Threading;
using System.Windows.Media.Imaging;
using Image = System.Drawing.Image;

namespace ES_Project
{
    //main class
    class Program
    {
        public static SerialPort mySerialPort = new
            SerialPort("COM8");
        public static String password = "password"; //to stop the
            alarm
        public static String date;
        public static String time;
        public static String hours;
        public static String minutes;
        public static String seconds;

        //for completeness
        public Program()
        {
        }

        //for not sending for every alarm a ton of mails
```

```csharp
private static int mailcounter = 0;

private BitmapImage _image;
public BitmapImage Image
{
    get { return _image; }
    set { Set(ref _image, value); }
}

private void Set(ref BitmapImage image, BitmapImage value)
{
    _image = value;
}

static void Main(string[] args)
{

    /* Thread to have the possibility to stop the program
    * at any time
    */
    Thread t = new Thread(Password);
    mySerialPort.PortName = "COM8";
    mySerialPort.BaudRate = 9600;
    mySerialPort.Open();
    t.Start();

    while (true)
    {

        //to notice if the alarm should start
        String dataFromArduino =
            mySerialPort.ReadLine().ToString();
        Console.WriteLine(dataFromArduino); //for checking
        if (dataFromArduino != null)
        {
```

12

```
/* getting the time when the alarm starts for the
 * protocol
 */
date = System.DateTime.Now.ToShortDateString();
hours = DateTime.Now.Hour.ToString();
minutes = DateTime.Now.Minute.ToString();
seconds = DateTime.Now.Second.ToString();

/* converting into Strings for writing it
 * into the protocol file
 */
time = hours + "h " + minutes + "min " + seconds
    + "sec";

//setting the name of the taken picture
String[] a = new String[1];
a[0] = "Snapshot";

//Mail and picture
if (mailcounter == 0)
{
    Snapshot(a);
    Mail();
    Console.WriteLine(date + time); //for checking
    mailcounter++;
}
DetectingProcesses(date, time);
Distraction();
            }


    }
}


/* for sending a mail with a picture as an attachment,
```

```
 * the picture is already stored on the computer,
 * here the mail is sent through yahoo,
 * the personal data (mail address and log in data)
 * is not filled in
 */
public static void Mail()
{
    MailMessage mail = new MailMessage();

    //mail sender (NOT FILLED IN)
    mail.From = new MailAddress("");

    //mail receiver (NOT FILLED IN)
    mail.To.Add("");
    mail.Subject = "Alarm"; //Mail title

    //Content of the mail
    mail.Body = "Someone tried to work on your pc";

    /* Picture, which is in this path stored, attached
     * to the mail
     */
    mail.Attachments.Add(new
        Attachment(@"C:\Users\mibet\source\repos\ES-Project\ES-Project\bir

    //SMTP Server from Yahoo
    SmtpClient client = new
        SmtpClient("smtp.mail.yahoo.com", 587);

    try
    {

        //log in data for the SMTP Server (NOT FILLED IN)
        System.Net.NetworkCredential nc = new
            System.Net.NetworkCredential("", "");
```

```
        client.Credentials = nc;

        //most of the mail systems acquire SSL
        client.EnableSsl = true;

        client.Send(mail);

        Console.WriteLine("Mail was sent");
    }
    catch (Exception ex)
    {
        Console.WriteLine("Error with sending\n\n{0}",
            ex.Message);
    }
}

//taking a picture
public static int Snapshot(String[] args)
{
    //variable declaration
    Webcam camera = new Webcam(new Size(320, 240), 30);
    Image captured_image = null;
    int counter = 0;
    String logfilename = "";

    try
    {
        /* Raise an exception if no command line parameter
         * has been passed to the program
         */
        if (args.Length != 1)
        {
            throw new FileNotFoundException();
        }
```

```csharp
//remove any extensions from target file name
int lastdot = -1;
lastdot = args[0].LastIndexOf(".");
if (lastdot != -1 &&
    !args[0].Substring(lastdot).Contains("\\"))
    args[0] = args[0].Substring(0, lastdot);

//asign the same log file name as the target file name
logfilename = new String(args[0].ToCharArray());

//Assign proper extensions to both filenames
if (!args[0].EndsWith(".jpg", true, null))
    args[0] = args[0] + ".jpg";

if (!logfilename.EndsWith(".log", true, null))
    logfilename = logfilename + ".log";

string curr_dir = Environment.CurrentDirectory;

//modify filenames to show absolute file paths
if (!args[0].Contains("\\"))
    args[0] = curr_dir + "\\" + args[0];

if (!logfilename.Contains("\\"))
    logfilename = curr_dir + "\\" + logfilename;

//start the camera
camera.Start();

/* Try capturing the image from the webcam 100 times
 * with sleeping 10 milliseconds before each try.
 */
do
{
    Thread.Sleep(10);
```

```csharp
        captured_image = camera.currentImage;
        counter++;
    } while (captured_image == null && counter <= 100);

    /* Processing has been finished
     * so successful or not, "stop" the camera
     */
    camera.Stop();

    /* If unsuccessful for all 100 times, raise an
        exception
     * or else process the captured image.
     */
    if (captured_image == null)
    {
        throw new Exception("Device time-out");
    }
    else
    {

        //write to both target & log files
        using (FileStream fs = new FileStream(args[0],
            FileMode.Create))
        {
            captured_image.Save(fs, ImageFormat.Jpeg);
            Console.WriteLine("Image stored at " +
                args[0]);
            WriteLog("Image stored at " + args[0],
                logfilename);
        }
    }
}
catch (FileNotFoundException)
{
```

```csharp
        Console.WriteLine("Error code 1 : Please specify two
            valid file-paths");
        return 1;
    }
    catch (ArgumentException)
    {
        Console.WriteLine("Error code 2 : Invalid path");
        WriteLog("Error code 2 : Invalid path", logfilename);
        return 2;
    }
    catch (NotSupportedException)
    {
        Console.WriteLine("Error code 3 : Path refers to a
            non-file device");
        WriteLog("Error code 3 : Path refers to a non-file
            device", logfilename);
        return 3;
    }
    catch (SecurityException)
    {
        Console.WriteLine("Error code 4 : Permission denied");
        WriteLog("Error code 4 : Permission denied",
            logfilename);
        return 4;
    }
    catch (DirectoryNotFoundException)
    {
        Console.WriteLine("Error code 5 : Directory not
            found");
        WriteLog("Error code 5 : Directory not found",
            logfilename);
        return 5;
    }
    catch (PathTooLongException)
    {
```

```csharp
            Console.WriteLine("Error code 6 : Path is too long");
            WriteLog("Error code 6 : Path is too long",
                logfilename);
            return 6;
        }
        catch (Exception ex)
        {
            Console.WriteLine("Error code 7 : " + ex.Message);
            WriteLog("Error code 7 : " + ex.Message, logfilename);
            return 7;
        }
        return 0;
    }


    /* for the snapshot method, writes where the image
     * is stored or writes an exception
     */
    private static void WriteLog(string message, string
        logfilepath)
    {
        try
        {
            using (StreamWriter writer =
                File.AppendText(logfilepath))
            {
                writer.WriteLine(message);
            }
        }
        catch (FileNotFoundException)
        {
            Console.WriteLine("Error code 1 : Please specify a
                valid log file-path");
        }
        catch (ArgumentException)
        {
```

```
            Console.WriteLine("Error code 2 : Invalid log path");
        }
        catch (NotSupportedException)
        {
            Console.WriteLine("Error code 3 : Log file-path
                refers to a non-file device");
        }
        catch (SecurityException)
        {
            Console.WriteLine("Error code 4 : Log file-path
                permission denied");
        }
        catch (DirectoryNotFoundException)
        {
            Console.WriteLine("Error code 5 : Log file-path
                directory not found");
        }
        catch (PathTooLongException)
        {
            Console.WriteLine("Error code 6 : Log file-path is
                too long");
        }
        catch (Exception ex)
        {
            Console.WriteLine("Error code 7 : " + ex.Message);
        }
}


//Example programs and Pictures are opened as a distraction
public static void Distraction()
{
    Process.Start(@"C:\Program Files\Microsoft
        Office\Office15\EXCEL.exe");
    Process.Start(@"C:\Program Files\Microsoft
        Office\Office15\WINWORD.exe");
```

```csharp
        Process.Start(@"C:\Program Files\Microsoft
            Office\Office15\POWERPNT.exe");
        Process.Start(@"C:\Program
            Files\Notepad++\notepad++.exe");
        Process.Start(@"C:\Users\mibet\OneDrive\Bilder\Desktop
            Hintergrnde\Auensee.jpg");
        Process.Start(@"C:\Users\mibet\OneDrive\Bilder\Desktop
            Hintergrnde\Auensee2.jpg");
        Process.Start(@"C:\Users\mibet\OneDrive\Bilder\Desktop
            Hintergrnde\Blatt3.jpg");
        Process.Start(@"C:\Users\mibet\OneDrive\Bilder\Desktop
            Hintergrnde\Blatt5.jpg");
        Process.Start(@"C:\Users\mibet\OneDrive\Bilder\Desktop
            Hintergrnde\Elch1.jpg");
        Process.Start(@"C:\Users\mibet\OneDrive\Bilder\Desktop
            Hintergrnde\Feld2.jpg");
        Process.Start(@"C:\Users\mibet\OneDrive\Bilder\Desktop
            Hintergrnde\Feld3.jpg");
        Process.Start(@"C:\Users\mibet\OneDrive\Bilder\Desktop
            Hintergrnde\Island7.jpg");
        Process.Start(@"C:\Users\mibet\OneDrive\Bilder\Desktop
            Hintergrnde\Island8.jpg");
        Process.Start(@"C:\Users\mibet\OneDrive\Bilder\Desktop
            Hintergrnde\Island9.jpg");
    }

    //to Stop the alarm on the Arduino
    public static void Stop()
    {
        mySerialPort.Write("1");
        Console.WriteLine("bertragen");
    }

    //for stopping the program on the computer
    public static void Password()
```

```
{
    while (true)
    {
        if (Console.ReadLine() == password)
        {
            Console.WriteLine("Alarm is going to be stopped");
            Stop();
            mySerialPort.Close();
            Console.WriteLine("Closed");
            System.Environment.Exit(0);
        }
        else
        {
            Console.WriteLine("Wrong password");
        }
        Thread.Sleep(3000);
    }
}

//For detecting the processes
public static void DetectingProcesses(String date, String
    time)
{
    Process[] processlist = Process.GetProcesses();
    for (int i = 1; i < processlist.Length; i++)
    {
        for (int j = i-1; j > -1; j--)
        {
            if (processlist[i]!= null && processlist[j]!=null
                && processlist[i].ProcessName ==
                processlist[j].ProcessName)
            {
                processlist[i] = null;
            }
        }
    }
```

```
}

/* Common backgroundprocesses hardcoded, so that they
 * don't appear in the protocol file
 */
ArrayList backgroundprocess = new ArrayList();
backgroundprocess.Add("igfxEM");
backgroundprocess.Add("valWBFPolicyService");
backgroundprocess.Add("jusched");
backgroundprocess.Add("IntelCpHeciSvc");
backgroundprocess.Add("HPSupportSolutionsFrameworkService");
backgroundprocess.Add("CiscoVideoGuardMonitor");
backgroundprocess.Add("System");
backgroundprocess.Add("Idle");
backgroundprocess.Add("svchost");
backgroundprocess.Add("ServiceHub.SettingsHost");
backgroundprocess.Add("ServiceHub.ThreadedWaitDialog");
backgroundprocess.Add("ServiceHub.DataWarehouseHost");
backgroundprocess.Add("conhost");
backgroundprocess.Add("RuntimeBroker");
backgroundprocess.Add("ES - Project");
backgroundprocess.Add("WUDFHost");
backgroundprocess.Add("SettingSyncHost");
backgroundprocess.Add("mDNSResponder");
backgroundprocess.Add("PerfWatson2");
backgroundprocess.Add("systray");
backgroundprocess.Add("WUDFHost");
backgroundprocess.Add("DPAgent");
backgroundprocess.Add("HPCommRecovery");
backgroundprocess.Add("taskhostw");
backgroundprocess.Add("SecurityHealthService");
backgroundprocess.Add("taskhostw");
backgroundprocess.Add("HotKeyServiceUWP");
backgroundprocess.Add("SystemSettings");
backgroundprocess.Add("csrss");
```

```
backgroundprocess.Add("SearchUI");
backgroundprocess.Add("wininit");
backgroundprocess.Add("Microsoft.ServiceHub.Controller");
backgroundprocess.Add("sedsvc");
backgroundprocess.Add("PresentationFontCache");
backgroundprocess.Add("SSScheduler");
backgroundprocess.Add("SearchProtocolHost");
backgroundprocess.Add("PresentationFontCache");
backgroundprocess.Add("sihost");
backgroundprocess.Add("fontdrvhost");
backgroundprocess.Add("DpAgent");
backgroundprocess.Add("SearchProtocolHost");
backgroundprocess.Add("fontdrvhost");
backgroundprocess.Add("esif_uf");
backgroundprocess.Add("LanWlanWwanSwitchingServiceUWP");
backgroundprocess.Add("ShellExperienceHost");
backgroundprocess.Add("E_YATIIUE");
backgroundprocess.Add("CxUtilSvc");
backgroundprocess.Add("igfxCUIService");
backgroundprocess.Add("hpqwmiex");
backgroundprocess.Add("wlanext");
backgroundprocess.Add("ServiceHub.Host.CLR.x86");
backgroundprocess.Add("LockApp");
backgroundprocess.Add("Flow");
backgroundprocess.Add("IntelAudioService");
backgroundprocess.Add("devenv");
backgroundprocess.Add("dllhost");
backgroundprocess.Add("WmiPrvSE");
backgroundprocess.Add("ScriptedSandbox64");
backgroundprocess.Add("javaw");
backgroundprocess.Add("SynTPHelper");
backgroundprocess.Add("ServiceHub.RoslynCodeAnalysisService32");
backgroundprocess.Add("CnxtNotify");
backgroundprocess.Add("backgroundTaskHost");
backgroundprocess.Add("winlogon");
```

```
backgroundprocess.Add("StandardCollector.Service");
backgroundprocess.Add("audiodg");
backgroundprocess.Add("SgrmBroker");
backgroundprocess.Add("RegSrvc");
backgroundprocess.Add("SgrmBroker");
backgroundprocess.Add("lsass");
backgroundprocess.Add("spoolsv");
backgroundprocess.Add("ctfmon");
backgroundprocess.Add("SearchFilterHost");
backgroundprocess.Add("LMS");
backgroundprocess.Add("MSASCuiL");
backgroundprocess.Add("MSBuild");
backgroundprocess.Add("ServiceHub.IdentityHost");
backgroundprocess.Add("HPNotifications");
backgroundprocess.Add("Eap3Host");
backgroundprocess.Add("Video.UI");
backgroundprocess.Add("dptf_helper");
backgroundprocess.Add("MicTray64");
backgroundprocess.Add("SearchIndexer");
backgroundprocess.Add("IAStorDataMgrSvc");
backgroundprocess.Add("hpMAMSrv");
backgroundprocess.Add("DpCardEngine");
backgroundprocess.Add("ApplicationFrameHost");
backgroundprocess.Add("SynTPEnhService");
backgroundprocess.Add("jhi_service");
backgroundprocess.Add("IAStorIcon");
backgroundprocess.Add("unsecapp");
backgroundprocess.Add("browser_broker");
backgroundprocess.Add("rundll32");
backgroundprocess.Add("rundll32");
backgroundprocess.Add("MicrosoftEdgeCP");
backgroundprocess.Add("dasHost");
backgroundprocess.Add("SynTPEnh");
backgroundprocess.Add("Memory Compression");
backgroundprocess.Add("vpnui");
```

```
backgroundprocess.Add("DpHostW");
backgroundprocess.Add("HPHotkeyNotification");
backgroundprocess.Add("VBCSCompiler");
backgroundprocess.Add("MsMpEng");
backgroundprocess.Add("HPJumpStartLaunch");
backgroundprocess.Add("CxMonSvc");
backgroundprocess.Add("ServiceHub.VSDetouredHost");
backgroundprocess.Add("EvtEng");
backgroundprocess.Add("dwm");
backgroundprocess.Add("IntelCpHDCPSvc");
backgroundprocess.Add("smss");
backgroundprocess.Add("ZeroConfigService");
backgroundprocess.Add("services");
backgroundprocess.Add("vpnagent");
backgroundprocess.Add("fpCSEvtSvc");
backgroundprocess.Add("ibtsiva");
backgroundprocess.Add("SkypeBridge");
backgroundprocess.Add("NisSrv");
backgroundprocess.Add("HPJumpStartBridge");
backgroundprocess.Add("SmartAudio3");
backgroundprocess.Add("alg");
backgroundprocess.Add("sedlauncher");
backgroundprocess.Add("Registry");
backgroundprocess.Add("Microsoft.Photos");
backgroundprocess.Add("SkypeBackgroundHost");

//to not write the date and time with all the processes
int counter = 0;
foreach (Process theprocess in processlist )
{
    if (theprocess != null)
    {
        String processName = theprocess.ProcessName;
        if (!backgroundprocess.Contains(processName))
        {   if (counter == 0)
```

```
                            {
                                Protocol.write(date + " " + time + "    " +
                                    theprocess.ProcessName);
                                counter++;
                            }
                            else
                            {
                                Protocol.write("
                                    " + theprocess.ProcessName);
                            }
                        }
                    }
                }
            }
        }
}
```

```
using System;
using System.Drawing;

using AForge.Video;
using AForge.Video.DirectShow;

namespace ImageCapture
{
    //class for using a camera
    class Webcam
    {

        //list of all videosources connected to the pc
        private FilterInfoCollection videoDevices = null;

        //the selected videosource
        private VideoCaptureDevice videoSource = null;
        private Size frameSize;
```

```
private int frameRate;

/* parameter accessible to outside world to
 * capture the current image
 */
public Bitmap currentImage;

public Webcam(Size framesize, int framerate)
{
    this.frameSize = framesize;
    this.frameRate = framerate;
    this.currentImage = null;
}

// get the devices names cconnected to the pc
private FilterInfoCollection getCamList()
{
    videoDevices = new
        FilterInfoCollection(FilterCategory.VideoInputDevice);
    return videoDevices;
}

//start the camera
public void Start()
{
    /*raise an exception in case no video device is found
     * or else initialise the video source variable with the
     * hardware device
     * and other desired parameters.
     */
    if (getCamList().Count == 0)
        throw new Exception("Video device not found");
    else
    {
        videoSource = new
```

```
            VideoCaptureDevice(videoDevices[0].MonikerString);
        videoSource.NewFrame += new
            NewFrameEventHandler(video_NewFrame);
        videoSource.DesiredFrameSize = this.frameSize;
        videoSource.DesiredFrameRate = this.frameRate;
        videoSource.Start();
    }
}


//dummy method required for Image.GetThumbnailImage() method
private bool imageconvertcallback()
{
    return false;
}


//eventhandler if new frame is ready
private void video_NewFrame(object sender,
    NewFrameEventArgs eventArgs)
{
    this.currentImage =
        (Bitmap)eventArgs.Frame.GetThumbnailImage(frameSize.Width,
        frameSize.Height, new
        Image.GetThumbnailImageAbort(imageconvertcallback),
        IntPtr.Zero);
}


//close the device safely
public void Stop()
{
    if (!(videoSource == null))
        if (videoSource.IsRunning)
        {
            videoSource.SignalToStop();
            videoSource = null;
        }
```

```csharp
        }
    }
}
```

```csharp
using System;
using System.Collections.Generic;
using System.IO;
using System.Linq;
using System.Text;
using System.Threading.Tasks;

namespace ES_Project
{
    //Class for creating and adding content on a text file
    class Protocol
    {
        static string path = @"C:\Users\mibet\Desktop";
        static string FileName = "Protocol.txt";
        public static void createFile()
        {
            string pathFile = Path.Combine(path, FileName);
            File.Create(pathFile).Close();
            File.WriteAllText(pathFile, "Date Time      Used
                Processes "); //first line of the file
        }

        //appending a new line to the textfile
        public static void write(String s)
        {
            string pathFile = Path.Combine(path, FileName);
            using (StreamWriter file = new StreamWriter(@pathFile,
                true))
            {
                file.WriteLine(s, true);
            }
```

30

```
            }
        }
    }
```
_____

7 Ressources

1.Latex [last seen 3 June 2019]:

   https://de.overleaf.com/learn/latex/How_to_Write_a_Thesis_in_LaTeX_(Part_5):
   _Customising_Your _Title_Page_and_Abstract
   https://tex.stackexchange.com/questions/7350/how-do-i-add-dots-in-toc

2. SerialPort [last seen 3 June 2019]:

   https://docs.microsoft.com/en-us/dotnet/api/system.io.ports.serialport.datareceived?redirected
   from=MSDN&view=netframework-4.8
   https://docs.microsoft.com/en-us/dotnet/api/system.io.ports.serialport.readline?redirectedfrom
   =MSDN&view=netframework-4.8#System_IO_Ports_SerialPort_ReadLine
   https://www.youtube.com/watch?v=TNLp5UV0dMI
   https://www.youtube.com/watch?v=m0u5PXrHK8o
   https://www.c-sharpcorner.com/UploadFile/c713c3/how-to-exit-in-C-Sharp/

3.Starting of an .exe-file [last seen 27 May 2019]:

   https://forum.arduino.cc/index.php?topic=308714.0

4.Tinkercad [last seen 27 May 2019]:

   https://www.tinkercad.com

5. Email [last seen 31 May 2019]:

   https://www.entwickler-ecke.de/topic_email+mit+c+versenden+und+Port+_116806.html&sid=f1ε
   https://www.pop3-imap-smtp.de/yahoo-mail/

6. Camera [last seen 31 May 2019]:

   https://code.google.com/archive/p/aforge/downloads?page=1
   https://github.com/mesta1/Recording-video-with-c-

https://www.codeproject.com/Questions/456777/Capturing-image-from-a-webcam

https://docs.microsoft.com/en-us/windows/uwp/audio-video-camera/basic-photo-video-and-audio-capture-with-mediacapture

https://docs.microsoft.com/en-us/dotnet/api/system.io.stream?view=netframework-4.8

https://docs.microsoft.com/en-us/dotnet/api/system.drawing.image?view=netframework-4.8

https://mycsharp.de/wbb2/thread.php?postid=3724686

https://csharp.hotexamples.com/examples/System.Drawing/Image/Save/php-image-save-method-examples.html

7. Protocol [last seen 4 June 2019]:

   https://www.tutorials.de/threads/c-aktuelles-datum-auslesen-und-als-string-wiedergeben.188090/

   https://social.msdn.microsoft.com/Forums/de-DE/a061b40e-eabf-4166-a407-d1c6611edc5f/uhrzeit-ohne-datum-anzeigen?forum=visualbasicde

   https://www.youtube.com/watch?v=ᵥCdRgZaRTw

8. Threads [last seen 5 June 2019]:

   https://o7planning.org/de/10553/die-anleitung-zu-csharp-multithreading-programmierung

9. Error [last seen 6 June 2019]:

   https://stackoverflow.com/questions/9194495/type-exists-in-2-assemblies